YOU'RE UNIQUE
& SO IS YOUR
PAIN

A Daily Reflections Journal for Lifelong Well-Being

DR. ANDREA FURLAN
MD, PhD, PM&R

For complete cataloguing information, see page 192.

Disclaimer

This book is a general guide only and should never be a substitute for the skill, knowledge, and experience of a qualified medical professional dealing with the facts, circumstances, and symptoms of a particular case.

The nutritional, medical, and health information presented in this book is based on the research, training, and professional experience of the author, and is true and complete to the best of their knowledge. However, this book is intended only as an informative guide for those wishing to know more about health, nutrition, and medicine; it is not intended to replace or countermand the advice given by the reader's personal physician. Because each person and situation is unique, the author and the publisher urge the reader to check with a qualified health-care professional before using any procedure where there is a question as to its appropriateness. A physician should be consulted before beginning any exercise program. The author and the publisher are not responsible for any adverse effects or consequences resulting from the use of the information in this book. It is the responsibility of the reader to consult a physician or other qualified health-care professional regarding his or her personal care.

Design and Production: PageWave Graphics Inc.
Editor: Kathleen Fraser
Author photo: Tim Fraser
Cover and interior illustrations: © Getty Images

We acknowledge the support of the Government of Canada.

Canadä

Published by Robert Rose Inc.
120 Eglinton Avenue East, Suite 800, Toronto, Ontario, Canada M4P 1E2
Tel: (416) 322-6552   Fax: (416) 322-6936
www.robertrose.ca

Printed and bound in Canada

1 2 3 4 5 6 7 8 9 CW 33 32 31 30 29 28 27 26 25

*To Laura Murphy, PharmD,
a true friend, cancer warrior
and exceptional professional
who helped so many people
conquer chronic pain*

CONTENTS

Why Should You Start a Chronic Pain Journal?

Life with chronic pain can be unpredictable. Not knowing what has caused your pain or what makes the pain worse can be very stressful. This can make you more cautious and afraid, and you start limiting your activities and stop doing things that you would normally do.

Journaling can also be good for helping you think about things you may want to share with others. For example, this book might be helpful if you are in a peer-support group. You can use it as a starting point to discuss at meetings.

Journaling can be a very effective tool in your pain management journey. Use this journal as a tool in your toolbox to understand and overcome your pain. You don't need to be a perfect writer or have great handwriting skills. This activity should not be a burden to you. You do not need to write every day.

This journal is *not* a diary for documenting your pain. In fact, I recommend that you don't journal your pain experiences.

I want my patients to forget pain and live their lives. I want them to unlearn pain and learn new skills that will help them to be more engaged in physical, mental and spiritual activities. This journal is meant to help you do that.

Each person is unique, and one person's pain journey will never be the same as someones else's journey. Chronic pain affects people differently, but it is important that each person understands how their life is impacted by chronic pain and develops their own strategies to minimize that impact.

Your toolbox

In this journal, I sometimes refer to your toolbox. Your toolbox should contain basic tools or strategies you can use for yourself when you feel pain. To make it easy to remember, I call them the 5Ms.

- **Mind-body therapies** such as mindfulness, meditation, hypnosis and relaxation
- **Movement** as a therapeutic intervention to treat pain and fix the malfunctioning pain system
- **Manual therapies** that you can do for yourself at home
- **Modalities** such as heat, cold and electrotherapy
- **Medication**, including anti-inflammatories, analgesics, muscle relaxants and topical compounds

Your goal is to increase your circles

Most people with chronic pain draw circles around their lives, and these circles become smaller and smaller.

The first circle is what they can do; the second includes meaningful people in their lives; the third is about who they are as a person.

When acute pain becomes chronic, the person starts a list of things they can't do. And as the list grows, the number of things they can do becomes very small.

Also, their circle of friends, relatives, colleagues and coworkers starts getting smaller as they limit their interactions with people.

And finally, they limit who they are because of their chronic pain. Their pain becomes their identity. They may feel useless, and think of themselves as a burden to others and to society.

The good news is, these circles are reversible! They are not written in stone. They can grow!

You too can increase your circles! You can achieve a satisfactory level of good health, no matter how intense your pain is now!

 Forget your pain and live your life!

Health is not the absence of disease. Health is a sense of physical, mental and spiritual well-being. Even people with serious health conditions can say that they are in good health when they are fully living their lives despite having diseases. Forget your pain and live your life!

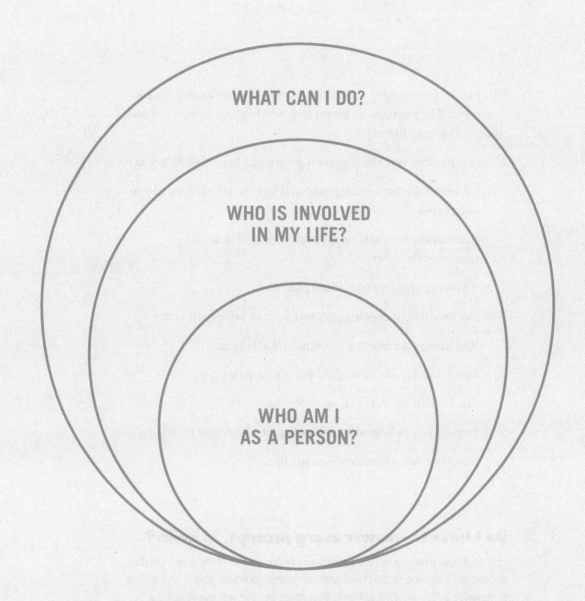

WHAT CAN I DO?

WHO IS INVOLVED
IN MY LIFE?

WHO AM I
AS A PERSON?

How to use your journal

This journal is organized with prompts, questions and space for you to respond. The prompts are meant to give you ideas, inspire you and guide you on your journey.

As you work your way through these prompts, I hope they help you to:

- Understand what has happened and how pain has changed you as a person.

- Learn about the mind-body connection and how one influences the other.

- Rediscover your strengths and potential.

- Document your ongoing progress and celebrate each victory.

- Recognize pain triggers, patterns and solutions.

- Learn and explore new possibilities to cope with pain.

- Track soothing and calming experiences.

- Prepare lists of helpful resources in case of a future pain flare.

- Develop inner resilience and enjoy life.

 Do I have to answer every prompt, in order?

I recommend that you do the prompts in order, as the order in which they appear will help you understand and track your journey. Also, I know from experience with my many patients that most people will eventually be affected by most of the issues included here, so I encourage you to respond to all of the prompts.

STOP JOURNALING IF THIS HAPPENS

- If you feel you are getting re-traumatized by the events that happened in your past. Get professional help. Seek a trauma-informed therapist.

- If you feel that journaling is not helping you to learn about yourself, to learn how pain modifies your body and mind, or how to understand your symptoms and how to manage them

- If you don't like this activity. Journaling is certainly not for everybody.

- If you notice worsening of your symptoms, mental health, quality of life, relationships or thoughts to harm yourself or someone else

1

Describe all of the significant painful episodes in your life

Let's start by describing what has happened to you since the beginning.

For some people, chronic pain started abruptly — after surgery, a car accident, a fracture or a nerve injury. For others, there was no inciting event — the pain was just insidious and accumulating.

On the opposite page, write down the first time you remember feeling pain. Go back to your childhood and list some episodes you remember when you had pain.

If you need more space, you can get extra paper. Don't add a lot of details; try to keep one line per episode. Your list may look something like this:

- About 3 years old, had ear pain

- About 8 years old, had chicken pox, with itching all over my body

- At age 10, broke my wrist

- From 13 to 24, had monthly menstrual cramps

- At age 18, had wisdom teeth removed

- Between 20 and 30, started having upper back pain

- At age 32, had a cesarian section

- At age 35, had a second cesarian section

- At age 45, had acute low back pain

- At age 47, had acute low back pain again

- At age 50, had shingles

This list happens to be my personal pain history. I'm glad that I didn't develop chronic pain from any of these episodes; however, one that keeps recurring is the pain in my upper back. More about that later.

Briefly describe all the significant pain episodes in your life, starting with the first one.

2

Write about one painful episode that did not become chronic

Think about your list of painful episodes that you wrote in Day 1, and choose one to write about. Try to select an episode from which you completely recovered, one that did not lead to chronic pain.

For my story, I would select the shingles. I had shingles when I was starting my summer vacation, and it kind of ruined my vacation, as I could not walk properly. The pain was in my buttock, the back of my thigh and the side of my leg. I noticed three different kinds of pain: one in the skin, like burning sensation, the second like a muscle pulling on my hamstrings, and the third, like electrical shocks running down my whole leg.

The doctor quickly diagnosed me as having shingles, and I began antiviral medications soon after the skin eruptions started. The doctor suggested pregabalin for pain relief, but I decided against it after I had a chat with my pharmacist about the pros and cons of a neuropathic pain medication. Instead, I applied a topical cream to the skin and used acetaminophen and ibuprofen when the pain was too intense.

My family was very supportive and understood that I had limitations during our vacation.

I was afraid of developing post-herpetic neuralgia, as I have seen many patients with this terrible type of chronic pain. I tried to keep doing the usual activities with my family, and not to worry about the pain. It lasted about six weeks and then started resolving. The skin was still sensitive for many months, but since then, I had not had any memory of pain or after-effects.

Write about the one painful episode you have chosen.

Try to remember how much it hurt, what people told you, what your fears were, how long it took to recover from that episode and what treatment you received.

3

Write about the beginning of your chronic pain

Now, I want you to think about to the origins of your chronic pain. Try to remember the first time that a healthcare professional told you that you have chronic pain. Chronic pain starts differently for each person.

Write about what caused your chronic pain.

What's the difference between acute and chronic pain?

Acute pain is pain that lasts less than three months.

Chronic pain is ongoing continuous pain that last for three months or longer and has passed the expected healing period.

How long ago did it start?

What were you told about your diagnosis?

What did you know about chronic pain at that time?

4

Describe your current state of health

"Health is defined as a physical, mental, social and spiritual well-being." — World Health Organization

How are you today?

This question is not just about pain — it is about you.

Describe your current health. What do you think your general state of health is?

You may write a list of all your health problems, but try to focus on how you perceive your health, or lack of health.

_____

_____

_____

_____

_____

_____

_____

_____

_____

Would you say you are healthy?

_____

_____

_____

_____

_____

_____

_____

_____

_____

_____

Health is not the absence of disease. It is a sense of physical, mental and spiritual well-being even in the presence of a serious health condition.

Are you trapped in a pain roundabout?

5

Do you see yourself trapped in a pain roundabout?

Have you ever heard of the pain roundabout? Adriaan Louw, author of *Why Do I Hurt?*, uses this image to describe what can happen to someone who has a hard time escaping their pain. A person may be trapped in a pain roundabout, like a car that is trapped in a traffic roundabout and cannot get out.

The things that keep people in the pain roundabout are increased fear, loss of hope, low motivation, fatigue, emotional stress, frustrations with the healthcare system, previous ineffective treatments and, most important, lack of knowledge of alternative options.

Are you trapped in a pain roundabout?

What is keeping you there?

_____

_____

_____

_____

_____

_____

_____

Can you see a way out for yourself?

_____

_____

_____

_____

_____

_____

_____

6

Is there a day of the week when your pain is more intense?

Some people notice they have migraines on Monday mornings, and that might be related to their work, which starts on Monday, and is where they have many demands or responsibilities.

Other people notice that pain is better on Mondays, and that is because their home situation may be too stressful, and that send signals to their brain that when they go away to work, they leave their problems at home.

Do you notice any pattern? If the mechanism of your pain is predominantly *nociplastic,* you will feel pain more intensely when your brain is sensing danger and unpleasant situations.

THREE MECHANISMS FOR PAIN

There are three mechanisms for pain: nociceptive, neuropathic and nociplastic.

1. NOCICEPTIVE PAIN is when the pain receptors are activated by some sort of injury, inflammation, damage, disease or lesion (for example, a skin cut, a fracture, appendicitis or an inflamed tooth). This is the most common type of acute pain.

2. NEUROPATHIC PAIN is when the nervous system is affected by a lesion or disease, such as a nerve compression (as in carpal tunnel syndrome), spinal cord injury, stroke or shingles.

3. NOCIPLASTIC PAIN is when there is a malfunction in the pain system, and the pain alarm system continues to be activated after the nociceptive or neuropathic pain has resolved. This is the most common type of chronic pain.

Do you notice any pattern in your own pain?

Are there any days of the week when your pain is regularly more intense?

Why do you think that is?

Can you feel pain without fear?

Pain itself can be a frightening experience. When we don't know what is causing the pain, or we imagine that something is severely broken, damaged or injured, the experience of fear could be worse than the pain itself.

Actually, people can experience intense pain just by thinking that their body is being threatened.

There is a famous story of a construction worker who stepped on a big nail that spiked though and was showing at the top of the boot. His coworkers brought him to emergency to remove the nail, as he was experiencing terrible pain. The doctors had to sedate him with benzodiazepine and give him a potent opioid painkiller. After removing the nail, they removed the boot and, to everyone's surprise, the nail had passed between the toes, not even scratching his skin. Does that mean that his pain was not real? Of course his pain was real.

In the case of nociplastic pain, if we reassure ourselves that there is no danger, and that the pain is an annoying signal of a false alarm, we can reduce our fear of pain.

If we deactivate the alarm system, the brain will calm down and eventually will learn that the situation is not dangerous and that the pain alarm can be turned off.

Reflect on how pain and fear are connected in your life. Write about it.

How is your happy meter?

Did you know that a lot of people with chronic pain spend hours, days, weeks, months and years trying to be 100% pain free? I have seen people who are still trying to reach that goal after 50 years of chronic pain, and they are so obsessed with this goal that they forget to live their lives.

It is important to keep living your life. Pursue activities and situations that you enjoy and that will keep you engaged with what is important to you.

Allow yourself to have fun, to enjoy your life and those around you.

ACT!

I sometimes recommend to my patients a type of psychotherapy called Acceptance and Commitment Therapy, or ACT. The basic principle of ACT is to live life with purpose and meaning, doing what is relevant to you.

Write about your happiness moments and what brings you joy.

Is your pain real?

Let's be clear once and for all. All pains are real. If you are feeling pain, then your pain is real.

Even with the latest scientific knowledge and technology, we still cannot see pain in a scan or lab test. Pain is what the person says it is. Pain is different for everyone, and even the same person feels pain differently depending on the body part, the circumstances, their previous experiences and their state of mind.

Chronic pain means that the pain is persisting beyond the period of healing. The main mechanism of chronic pain is nociplastic pain. This means that pain sensation is coming from the "pain system" and not the muscles, tendons, bones, joints, organs or nerves.

Because doctors don't know much about the pain system and nociplastic pain, they end up explaining that the "pain is in your head."

There is no difference between physical pain and emotional pain. All pains are physical and emotional. Even nociplastic pain is physical, but the biological mechanism is not in the peripheral tissues; instead, the abnormal biological mechanisms are in the pain system, which is mainly in the brain.

Is your pain real?

Has anyone ever told you that your pain is all in your head?

What do people mean when they say "pain is in the brain"?

Write about your understanding of this statement.

How do you imagine
others perceive you
and your pain?

10

What will others see, hear or feel?

Imagine that you have traveled to a different country. You meet a person you have never seen before, someone who has never before met you. This person is observing you when you are having a painful episode.

How will another person describe what they see, hear or feel when observing you?

_____

_____

_____

_____

_____

_____

_____

How do you imagine others perceive you and your pain?

_____

_____

_____

_____

_____

_____

_____

_____

_____

_____

Do you have any daily habits?

Think about your daily routine. What are some things that you do everyday? Think especially about habits that are soothing or calming to your body and or mind.

When I asked this question on social media, these were some of the habits that respondents shared:

- Warm showers or baths
- Warm tea
- Leaning into pleasant sensations
- Daily exercises
- Exercises combined with time in nature
- Painting
- Knitting
- Listening to an audiobook or music
- Singing — belting it out
- Playing an instrument
- Crosswords
- Playing a video game

What is your daily routine?

Make a list. Try to write one item per line.

When you are done, circle the habits that are calming and soothing to you.

Feel-good list

What do you do to feel good?

For this journal entry, I want you to make a list. This is not a list of things to reduce your pain, so do not include anything that is related to painkillers or analgesics.

The focus should not be on your pain but instead on actions that make you feel good in general, especially things that you can do to improve your overall health and well-being. Remember to think of these actions as tools in your toolbox. Do not include anything that is unhealthy, even if it something you do to feel good, for example, smoking.

Make a list of things you do to feel good.

Write one action per line.

_____

_____

_____

_____

_____

_____

_____

_____

_____

_____

_____

_____

_____

_____

_____

_____

Now, look at your list above and circle your favorite three things.

Dear me, I would like to tell you this

Write a letter to yourself.

Start with Dear _____ (your name).

You can just follow your gut and start writing, but here are some suggestions in case you need them.

- What things do you appreciate about yourself?

- What makes you unique and special?

- How do you respect and treat yourself? Some people have more patience and respect for others than they do for themselves. Is this your case?

- How do you make people around you feel about themselves?

- How do you react to other people's problems?

- Give yourself some words of encouragement.

Dear me,

14

Dear me, I would like to offer you some advice

Write another letter to yourself, this time with some advice.

Start with Dear _____ (your name).

This is similar to the previous exercise, but now, give yourself advice related to your overall health and well-being.

- What would you tell yourself if you were another person?

- What guidance or counsel would you offer?

You may write a list of health-related suggestions or just explore and expand on a single piece of advice.

Dear me,

What makes you precious?

A tree is made *strong* and *useful* by many seasons of winds, rain and sun.

A diamond is made *precious* by the bonds created on each carbon atom when the carbon is pressed and exposed to immense heat.

Clay becomes *beautiful* and *useful* when shaped and fired by the potter's creativity and hard work. There is a story in the Old Testament about the potter and the clay. It tells how the clay is molded in the potter's hand to become beautiful and useful, and the clay has no say in the process.

Write about what makes you strong, useful, precious and beautiful..

16

A small victory

Do you like celebrations? I am all-in when the motive is to celebrate. Anniversaries and birthdays are often marked as big achievements in life. But what about the small achievements? Why not celebrate them too?

Think about a situation where you accomplished something good related to your health. It might seem small to you, but it is still considered an achievement. Why not celebrate it?

What was it?

When did you achieve it?

How did you achieve it?

Who helped you to achieve it?

Did you celebrate that small victory? How?

Celebrating a victory can be a simple act of kindness to yourself, such as going out for dinner, buying a new pair of shoes, taking a picture or posting on social media about your accomplishment.

Dear body, I would like to tell you this

Your body is unique. Even if you have an identical twin, I bet your relatives and your friends can distinguish between the two of you. Your body size, your skin color, your hair, your eyes, your voice — they are all unique. There is no one like you.

Like it or not, yours is the body you have. Some people might try to change it, but it is still your own body. When you hate your body, it will hate you back. When you love your body, it will love you back.

Remember that the mind is contained in the body. There is no such thing as mind and body. They are all one thing.

Write a letter to your body.

Start with Dear body.

Here are some suggestions:

- Dear body, I have noticed that when you _____ (do this), the pain appears in the _____ (body part).

- I like when you _____ (do this), because the pain _____ (what happens).

- I would like you to _____ (do something) when I _____ (do something).

- How do you feel when I _____ (do something) to you?

- I appreciate you. Thank you for _____ (something good that your body does for you).

- I want to take good care of you. I will start _____ (a new habit for self-care).

Dear body,

18

Fear of change

"Times change and we with time."

— 16th century English proverb

Our brain tends to seek what is familiar and to avoid the unexpected and unpredictable. The brain always returns to what it is used to. It has a comfort zone — even if that zone is pain.

If you have had pain for many months or years, that is the new normal for your brain. Because your brain has adapted to it, it will be resistant to change and to thinking differently.

Be patient, because healing takes time. You cannot make a wound heal faster. You will not see change right away. Let your brain adapt to a new normal.

Talk to your brain about change.

What do you want to change? Do you want to stop some thoughts? Acknowledge and treat some emotions? Create new habits?

_____

_____

_____

_____

_____

_____

_____

_____

_____

_____

_____

Are you afraid of change?

What are your expectations for change? What do you think will happen?

What changes would you need to make if you had no more pain?

What drains your battery?

**"In trouble to be troubled, is to have
your trouble doubled."**

— Daniel Defoe, *The Farther Adventures of Robinson Crusoe*, 1719

Like apps opened in your cell phone, energy-draining emotions — worry, anger, resentment, unforgiveness and bitterness — are draining your battery.

Little by little, these emotions are silent killers, constantly draining your happiness, energy and healing powers. These losses combine and accumulate to weaken your well-being.

You need to do a daily emotional check-up and close all the "emotion apps" that are open in your mind.

One of the things that drains my energy is watching the news on TV. I stopped doing that many years ago. I realized that the images and videos that I was watching were disturbing my sleep, robbing my peace and joy in life. I still get news updates on the radio while I'm preparing breakfast, but that is it. I know what is going on around me. And since I stopped watching TV news, my quality of life and productivity has been much better.

Write about the negative emotion "apps" that are open in your mind.

Make a list of the sources of these energy drainers.

These can include television, radio, news, social media, neighbors, coworkers, family members or friends.

20

Are you making this mistake?

Don't find out the hard way.

Do an inventory of your daily activities. Is there any mistake that you make over and over again?

Select something that is affecting your health and aggravating your pain. This could be related to your sleep routine, what you eat, the substances that you put in your body (for example, alcohol, smoke), the people that you allow to influence you and your health, or something else.

If you find more than one mistake you make regularly, choose just one to write about today.

Understanding your mistakes is an important first step in overcoming them.

Write about a mistake that you make over and over. What is it?

_____

_____

_____

Why is that you keep doing this thing?

_____

_____

_____

How do you know it is a mistake?

_____

_____

_____

_____

What do you need in order to stop doing it repeatedly?

_____

_____

_____

_____

_____

Do you need any professional help?

_____

_____

_____

_____

_____

How long do you need to stop doing this thing?

_____

_____

_____

_____

_____

_____

_____

_____

_____

_____

On a scale from zero to ten, how confident are you
that you can stop making this mistake?

0 1 2 3 4 5 6 7 8 9 10

0 = Not confident   10 = Extremely confident

Repetition to make new synapses

"Repeat an action and you create a new habit. Repeat a good habit and you build your character."

Our brain doesn't change if it is not stimulated.

A person doesn't learn how to drive by being a passenger for many years. It is only when you sit in the driver's seat and press the gas pedal that you feel how difficult it is to control your arms, legs, eyes, sounds, people and cars and someone giving you instructions. But after weeks, months and years of practice, you have become good at this, and you can even drive on autopilot, which takes very little effort from your brain.

That is because the synapses that you created in your brain when you were learning to drive have been reinforced. With repetition, they became stronger and stronger, and you no longer need to make an effort for the electrical impulses to travel from one side of your brain to the other and to the whole body.

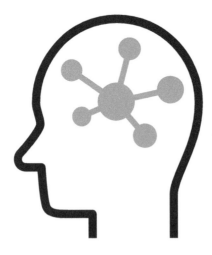

Write about new habits you want to develop that will help you to conquer chronic pain.

_____

_____

_____

_____

_____

_____

_____

_____

How will you develop these new habits?

_____

_____

_____

_____

_____

_____

_____

_____

_____

_____

_____

22

Your brain believes what you tell it

Think about what you think about. What do you regularly tell yourself? There are many thousands of thoughts that cross your mind every day.

Are your thoughts like this? *I can't do this! I can't go there! I don't like this! I am seriously damaged! I have something very bad! I am not worthy! I am useless! I am hopeless!*

Your brain is listening, and since you are an authority on your own life, your brain believes what you tell it. What if instead you told yourself, *I can do this! I can go there. I like this. I am healthy. I am well. I am worthy. I am useful. I have hope.*

I once had a patient who had pain in her wrist for more than three years. She had seen all kinds of specialists and everyone concluded that her wrist was healthy, but she continued to have wrist pain. During the consult with our team, she repeated this sentence at least 20 times: "I can't use this wrist for anything." I asked her to think about what she was saying, and go home and repeat a different sentence 20 times per hour: "My wrist is normal, and every doctor that I've seen has confirmed that my wrist is healthy." When I saw her in follow-up many months later, she was moving and using her wrist, hand and arm normally.

Write at least 10 things that you repeat frequently related to your pain.

These can be thoughts or sentences that you speak.

_____

_____

_____

_____

_____

_____

_____

_____

_____

_____

_____

Now rewrite your 10 statements in the opposite way, in a positive way.

Repeat your new phrases more often every day until your brain starts doing
it automatically. Remember, you are creating new synapses in your brain.

_____

_____

_____

_____

_____

_____

_____

_____

_____

_____

_____

23

Do not track the weather

Why not track the weather?

- It is useless, because it is very rarely a cause of pain flares unless you have a piece of metal in your body or an inflammation that is affected by barometric pressure.

- You can't do anything about it and it leaves you powerless and in the hands of a mysterious force of nature.

- It is easier to blame the weather than your own emotions, thoughts and attitudes. It becomes an excuse.

Instead, track these:

- Your mood, including stress and anxiety

- Your thoughts, including fears, anger, shame, guilt, frustration

- Sleep

- Movement

- Interactions with other people, relationships

- Pain-soothing activities

Pick one thing to track and record it for 7 days here.

I remember one of my patients who recognized her pain flares were related to her relationships. Tracking is how she found that out. These are examples of what she tracked.

MONDAY: I didn't see anyone, my children didn't call me, nobody sent me a personal message on social media. I felt alone and abandoned. My headache was very bad. I thought my head was going to explode.

TUESDAY MORNING: My son called and asked me how I was doing. After lunch, my neighbor knocked on my door and asked if I wanted to go outside. We went out together. My headache was much better.

WEDNESDAY: I called my sister and had an argument with her. My back pain flared up.

THURSDAY: My back and headache are really bad. I didn't want to talk or see anyone.

FRIDAY: I had to call the doctor because my back pain was so bad. The doctor told me to go to her office and she examined me. She said I was fine.

SATURDAY: The back pain and headaches were minimal.

SUNDAY: I went to church, spoke to many people there, we went out for lunch with some friends. I felt pain but it didn't bother me so much.

24

Do not track your calories; instead, track this

What you eat has a lot to do with how you feel pain. However, you did not suddenly have a flare-up because one day you had a hot dog (which is an ultra processed food). The problem is when your regular diet consists of junk food, lacks essential nutrients such as omega 3s, vitamins, minerals and water, and contains a lot of toxic substances such as preservatives, sweeteners, antimicrobials, antioxidants, trans fats, sugars, salt, caffeine and alcohol.

Tracking calories is not the way to reduce your pain. Instead, write about how you can improve your eating habits.

What are you doing to eliminate junk food and to improve your eating habits and your nutrition?

What are you doing to consume less sugary drinks, caffeine or alcohol and drink more water?

_____

_____

_____

_____

_____

_____

What are the barriers that you have to eating nutritious meals?

_____

_____

_____

_____

_____

_____

How will you feel after you make these changes?

_____

_____

_____

_____

_____

_____

_____

25

Embrace boredom

For most people, life has become hectic and busy. We rarely have downtime or rest time. The brain was not designed to be constantly overstimulated. Chronic pain may be the language your brain is using to inform you that it needs some downtime.

Today, do something that is monotonous and repetitive. In other words, spend some time doing an activity that you consider boring.

Choose something that requires very little mental energy for you. Do it for a few minutes or a few hours. Do not listen to or watch anything else. Just do that one activity, focused on one thing only.

Each person is different, so what might require little mental energy for you will be a high-energy activity for another person. Here are some suggestions.

- Organizing a drawer
- Folding towels and linens
- Painting a fence
- Walking in circles around the block
- Weeding your garden
- Knitting or crocheting
- Lane swimming
- Doing the dishes
- Solving a jigsaw puzzle

When you have completed the "boring" activity, write about your experience. Where did your mind take you?

_____

_____

_____

_____

_____

_____

_____

_____

_____

_____

_____

How does it feel to be alone with yourself? Did you enjoy the company?

_____

_____

_____

_____

_____

_____

_____

_____

_____

_____

_____

_____

26

Who are you trying to impress?

Think about the people in your life right now.

Write freely about them here. Write what you would like to say but feel you cannot say directly to them. Sometimes those thoughts ruminate inside our heads and they need an escape valve.

(If you think they may read this journal and you want to keep this away from them, get a scrap of paper or open a digital file and shred the paper or delete the file afterward.)

Who has influence over you?

_____

_____

_____

_____

_____

_____

Do you feel a need to impress them?

_____

_____

_____

_____

_____

_____

_____

_____

Do you fear their opinion?

Do you depend on them financially, emotionally or physically?

Are you able to openly express your opinions when these people are with you?

"There is no greater agony than bearing
an untold story inside you." — Maya Angelou

27

Write about the present

Should you write about your past, present or future?

My advice is, don't dwell in your past. You can think about how your past has shaped you, but write about your present.

Although the future may worry you, don't write about it.

Live in the present.
Today, write about
today only.

Adapted from Dan Buglio, *Pain Free You*

Write about today. How is your day going?

28

Write about the why,
not the what

"It is during our darkest moments that we must focus to see the light." — Aristotle Onassis

Now, instead of listing your emotions or your pain, try to write about why you are feeling the way you do.

This book is not meant to be a place to wallow in anger. If someone has hurt you in your past, write about it, but do not marinate in the misery juice. Let the emotion come out, but do not stay in that emotional soup. Move on. Let it go. Forgive and turn the page.

What you need to focus on is, what did that experience teach you? How has that experience shaped your personality? Did it help you to become more resilient, appreciative and kind?

If your experiences have made you a bitter, angry and resentful person, I suggest you seek professional counseling so you can talk about this.

Why do you feel the way you do?

_____

_____

_____

_____

_____

_____

_____

_____

_____

What lessons have you learned from experiences when you have felt hurt?

_____

_____

_____

_____

_____

_____

_____

_____

_____

_____

_____

29

Why is that pain stuck in that part of your body?

Think about your body. Does it feel as if there is a particular part of your body where the pain is stuck?

There might be an explanation for why one part of your body always hurts, and the explanation might be a psychological trauma that occurred in the past.

I have had people with chronic pelvic pain tell me that they had a history of sexual abuse, and that is why their pain is stuck in their pelvis.

Not every pain is caused by psychological trauma, but some are, and the pain doesn't resolve until the psychological trauma is resolved.

Write about why you think a particular part of your body is more vulnerable to pain.

Is there a part your body where the pain is stuck? Where is it?

_____

_____

_____

_____

Did anyone in your family have pain in that part of their body too? Any coworker? Any celebrity or influencer that you admire?

_____

_____

_____

_____

What does the body part where you feel pain represent to you?

_____

_____

_____

_____

_____

_____

_____

_____

_____

_____

_____

When you finish writing, give yourself a few minutes for self-compassion, gratitude and acceptance.

_____

30

Rewire your brain

No matter what your age, your brain can change. This is called neuroplasticity. Actually, any part of our body can change — our muscles, our bones, cartilage, skin and so on. We call this bioplasticity.

The brain just needs stimulation. If the stimulus is good, the brain changes for the better; if the stimulus is bad, it changes for the worse. And this is how we learn. It may take longer as you age, but the brain is plastic — meaning it can be changed — and we need this neuroplasticity to overcome chronic pain. You are capable of creating new synapses!

You can demonstrate this to your brain.

Do something that you have never done before in your life. Expose your brain to something new.

Here are some suggestions:

- Write with your non-dominant hand.
- Write looking at the paper in a mirror.
- Walk backwards.
- Write a poem.
- Compose a song.
- Imitate an animal.
- Cook a food that you have never cooked before.
- Draw a picture.
- Do a movement that you've never done before.
- Learn a new dance move.
- Speak some words in a language that is new to you.
- Memorize some phone numbers.

Now, write about the experience.

What did you do? Did you like or hate it? Was it easy or difficult?

_____

_____

_____

_____

_____

_____

_____

What did your brain tell you while you were doing it?

Did it tell you *This is stupid, or What a waste of time, or Look how disgusting this is?*

Those are common messages your brain will send you when you try to use neuroplasticity to overcome your chronic pain.

_____

_____

_____

_____

_____

_____

_____

_____

_____

_____

31

Use neuroplasticity to conquer chronic pain

Before you complete this activity, do the activity from the day before (Day 30).

In the previous prompt, you showed yourself that your brain is plastic because you were able to learn something new. Now, you can learn to do something new to overcome chronic pain.

Here are some examples of activities or habits you can start:

- Retrain your neural pathways.
- Control your emotions.
- Improve your sleep efficiency.
- Eat nutritious meals.
- Increase your social network.
- Rely less on drugs, injections and procedures.
- Put more tools in your toolbox.
- Work toward your goals.

Write about some new activities or habits that you will practice to promote neuroplasticity, to overcome your chronic pain.

32

Mindful eating

Choose a piece of food that you will eat today. It could be a fruit,
a vegetable or a nut. Go to a quiet place where you will not be interrupted
and eat it there.

Write about this one item of food. What is it?

Where did it come from? Do you know where it was grown?

What was its shape?

What color was it?

Write about its smell.

What was its texture?

What size was it?

How soft or firm was it?

How did it taste?

What nutrients did it contain?

How good is it for your body?

Now, express gratitude for this food.

33

Make a new friend

**"If you want to go fast, go alone. If you want
to go far, go together."** — African proverb

Are you always around the same group of people? When was the last time
you talked to someone you just met for the first time?

Many of my patients with chronic pain reduce their circle of friends.

*Today I want you to make a new friend. And have a conversation
with them.*

Find someone you have never had a conversation with before. That person
could be a neighbor, a grocery clerk, a random person in the park, someone
from the gym or a coworker.

Write about the experience of making a new friend. How did you feel?

Use lots of different words to describe your emotions and feelings related to this
encounter. Was it enjoyable, awkward, interesting, frustrating? Did you feel judged,
threatened, afraid, angry, happy, relieved, inspired?

Now, write about what you learned about yourself.

Did you learn that your circle can be larger than it is? That other people can enrich your life? That other people have problems too?

_____

_____

_____

_____

_____

_____

_____

_____

_____

_____

_____

_____

_____

_____

_____

_____

_____

_____

_____

_____

_____

_____

Did you know?

Did you know that our brain makes new synapses when we are connected with other people? It releases neurotransmitters that prevent diseases and even combat cancer.

34

What makes your muscles tense?

"Your body hears everything your mind says."

— Naomi Judd

Did you know that our muscles react to mental stress?

For some people, like me, it is the muscles of the neck and top of the shoulder. For others, it is the lower back muscles; for others, it could be the facial, jaw, arms, legs, chest, abdominal or pelvic muscles.

Write about what you notice about your muscles when you are under stress.

Where do you notice tension?

35

Focus more on your life and less on your pain

"Every day may not be good, but there's something good in every day." — Alice Morse Earle

When your brain is focused on your life goals, it has less time to be focused on pain.

No matter if you are 8 or 88, everyone should have goals, short-term or long-term goals. No goal is too small.

What are your goals?

- Visit a relative who lives far away, who you don't see for a long time?

- Learn a new skill, get a degree, find a new job?

- Hold your grandkids, or cook a nice meal for your family?

SMARTer Goals

Think of your goals as SMARTer: Specific, Measurable, Achievable, Relevant, Time Evaluable and Revisable. For example, someone who wants to move more might write this: "I will play soccer with my kids twice a week to add some physical exercise to my life."

Write about your life goals.

36

Motion is lotion

You have probably heard that exercise is good for you, but when you are in pain it is hard to think about doing any exercise. Even worse, if exercise aggravates your pain, your brain will tell you to stop.

How can you keep exercising on a regular basis? If you reduce the exercise you do, your body will think that that is the new normal and will resist when you try to do more.

This then becomes one of those frustrating circles of cause and effect that happens especially in the lives of people with chronic pain. It needs work to get out of it.

Stop saying "I can't do exercises," and replace that by saying "What kind of exercise can I do today?"

You need to remember that hurt does not mean harm. Forget the old saying "wear and tear" and replace it with "motion is lotion."

Are you afraid of exercise? Why?

What do you think about the saying "motion is lotion"?

Write about how you can keep exercising regularly, even when you have chronic pain.

What kind of exercise will you do today?

37

Write about another person

Today I want you to write about someone else who has conquered chronic pain.

Do you know someone who has conquered chronic pain? Someone who lives a fulfilling life despite having a condition that causes chronic pain?

If you don't, they are not hard to find. They are all over the internet. If you don't know where to start, go to my YouTube channel at https://www.youtube.com/@DrAndreaFurlan/podcasts. I've interviewed a couple of them.

Select one person who has conquered chronic pain and write about their life story.

Find someone similar to you or with a similar pain history.

You may summarize the main points in their healing journey. You may not agree with everything that they have done or everything that they say. Document what you hear and what you see. Pay attention to their body language and facial expressions.

38

Are you afraid of what the doctor has told you about your pain?

Many doctors and therapists are unaware of the differences between acute and chronic pain. They think that chronic pain is the same as acute pain, but it just lasts longer.

The truth is that acute pain is generally a signal of an injury, a lesion or a tissue that is structurally damaged or threatened. However, once the threat is removed, the pain signals should have turned off, but in some people they have not. The body continues triggering the alarm of pain because it doesn't know that the danger has ended. This is why many people develop chronic pain.

That means that chronic pain, although it is very real and tormenting, it is usually not a sign of danger to the body. It is a faulty alarm signal.

So, when doctors treat chronic pain the same way they treat acute pain they may use words like:

- "Your bones have been destroyed by arthritis."

- "Your body doesn't heal well."

- "You will need to take this medication for the rest of your life."

- "You have disc bulges in many segments of your spine."

Once you learn that you can turn off the danger signals, the alarm system will stop and the pain will go away.

But if you keep thinking about the erroneous messages the doctors have told you in the past, your mind will not disconnect from these messages.

Acute pain from structural damage is similar to a hardware problem in a malfunctioning computer.
Chronic pain can be compared to a software problem, where the computer is malfunctioning but there is no structural damage.

Make a list of the pessimistic messages you have received from your doctors or therapists in the past. Rewrite the list in an optimistic fashion.

Here is an example:

"Your body is getting old and your pain will just get worse and worse," versus "My body is resilient and is adapting to the environment around me."

39

Worry about the future

"We are more often frightened than hurt, and we suffer more from imagination than in reality."

— Lucius Seneca, AD 65

What good is worrying about the future? Will you change anything if you worry more? Do you think that if you worry about the future, you will change it?

Actually, the opposite is true. If you live in the present, you will be more productive, attentive, creative and happier.

Try to write 5 good reasons why a person should worry about the future.

Think about the differences between planning for the future and worrying about the future.

Now, write 5 reasons why a person should not worry about the future.

40

High or low pain tolerance?

How do you tolerate pain?

People have different pain tolerances. The interesting thing is that the same person can have a different pain tolerance depending on:

- the period in their lives (childhood, teenage years, young adults, older adults)

- the time of the day (morning, afternoon, night)

- what is happening around them (war zone, car accident, tragic event)

- who is by their side (a loved one or a torturer)

- the opinion they have about what is causing the pain (is this cancer, appendicitis or a heart attack?)

But what is even more interesting is that the same person will have different pain tolerances to different kinds of stimulus. A person may be more tolerant to a visible cut in their skin, but less tolerant to a minor muscle sprain in the back. Or they can tolerate a kidney stone well (because they know it is passing soon), but not a migraine (because they don't know when it is going to end).

Describe your pain tolerance levels.

Do you feel you have a high or low pain tolerance?

How does your pain tolerance change?

41

Look in the mirror

"Talk to yourself like you would to someone you love." — Brené Brown

What do you see when you look in the mirror? Describe what you see.
Rediscover your strengths and potential.

_____

_____

_____

_____

_____

_____

_____

_____

_____

_____

_____

_____

_____

_____

_____

_____

_____

42

What does your age mean to you?

**"Some day you will be old enough to
start reading fairy tales again." — C.S. Lewis**

Reflect on what you believe about aging and ageism. Do you feel that
your age is a factor that hinders your ability to live fully and happily?
Why is that?

_____

*What did you hear about older adults when you were younger?
Did someone influence your perspective of aging when you were
a child, teenager or younger adult?*

_____

_____

_____

_____

_____

_____

_____

_____

_____

_____

**Ageism is prejudice or
discrimination based
on a person's age.**

_____

_____

_____

Did you have a good or bad role model in the older adults in your life? Were they active and happy or were they miserable and bitter?

What does your age mean to you? What is "old" to you?

What do you want to become when you are old?

43

If your body was different

"By changing the story you tell in your head, you can change your pain."

CHANGING THE STORY

I once had a patient who had a problem with her self-image. She was in her twenties, had perfect health, and when we examined her, we could not find anything wrong. Yet she had pain all over her back, from her neck to lumbar spine. Everything hurt. We asked her what she thought was the cause of her pain and she answered, "My spine is all misaligned, the bones don't stick together, my connective tissue is weak and I can't do enough exercises to fix this." She had been told by various chiropractors and physiotherapists that she needed regular adjustments and extensive exercises for the rest of her life. We had to spend a lot of time explaining to her that her spine was perfectly aligned and very strong, and that the story she was playing in her head was sending danger signals to her brain and causing the pain.

Reflect on your self-esteem. What do you like or don't like about your physical body?

_____

_____

_____

_____

_____

_____

Is there a story about your body that you play in your head that could be sending danger signals to your brain? What is it?

_____

_____

_____

_____

_____

_____

Do you think you would be happier if your body was different? Why?

_____

_____

_____

_____

_____

_____

_____

44

Practice silence

> "Conversation enriches the understanding,
> but solitude is the school of genius."
>
> — Edward Gibbon,
>
> *The Decline and Fall of the Roman Empire, 1776–88*

Solitude is different from loneliness.

Loneliness is a state of being alone because you don't have friends or company, and is accompanied by emotions of sadness, hopelessness, abandonment and shame.

Solitude is a choice and it is a healthy habit. It takes personal discipline to be alone, solely in the company of yourself. It allows meaningful self-reflection and personal growth. No radio, no TV, no computer, no magazine, no other distraction. Just you and yourself.

Describe what you feel when you are by yourself in silence.

Do you spend more time in the past, present or future?

Do you think more about yourself or about others?

Are you able to focus on only a few thoughts, or do you have a thousand thoughts running in different directions?

45

Mind fasting

Have you ever tried to fast for a few hours or days? Not ingesting food for a period of time can provide rest to your digestive system.

Have you tried mind fasting? With mind fasting, you don't feed your mind with any kind of stimulation. You abstain from news, music, reading, talking or learning anything.

Think about the overstimulation that your brain receives throughout the day. Is it too much? What kind of food are you feeding your brain? Is it healthy? Do you listen to bad news, violent movies or fights? What kind of music do you listen to?

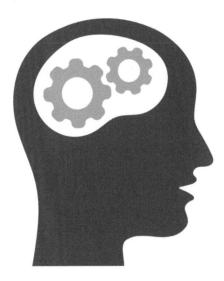

Try mind fasting for a few minutes.

You may go to a place with very little stimulation or sit in a chair and look at the same scene. It could be a beach, a tree, a building or a window.

If you are able to, instead of doing this exercise for a few minutes, try for a few hours or days.

Reflect on some changes you need to make in how you feed your mind.
Write about this.

46

Practice mindfulness

Mindfulness is the opposite of emptying your mind.

It is filling your mind with a thought or an experience, and focusing only on that for the duration of the practice. You do not allow the mind to wander to other places.

It includes observing the thought or experience without judging it as good or bad, without analyzing it. Just observing and staying focused on the activity.

For this exercise, bring your focus to a thought or experience of your choosing.

Try a mindful practice for about 5 to 10 minutes.

It can be a mindfulness meditation, mindful eating, mindful walking, mindful exercise or something else.

Then write about it here.

If you are a novice at practicing mindfulness, write about how easy or difficult it was. If you an experienced mindfulness practitioner, write about how long can you do a practice and the benefits it brings to you.

47

What is the danger?

**"Journaling allows every source of stress,
in my mind or my body, to have an outlet."**
— Carolyn Zepf

When your brain detects danger around you, it sounds the alarm, and the body may translate that alarm as pain.

Think about situations that make your pain worse. Is it a fight with your partner? Is it a worry about your children? Is it a financial problem you are facing? Is it a legal battle with someone who has injured you?

The sympathetic and parasympathetic autonomous nerve systems are two opposite systems we have embedded in our central and peripheric nervous system. They oppose each other. The *sympathetic nervous system* reacts to danger by creating a fight or flight response. The *parasympathetic nervous system* is active when we are in a safe zone, and it is known as the rest, digest and healing system.

Write about situations that your brain may detect as danger, when, as a consequence, your sympathetic nervous system will be on high alert.

_____

_____

_____

_____

_____

_____

_____

_____

When you have a pain flare, do you notice other signs of sympathetic activity?

Examples are accelerated heart beat, sweats, tremors, agitation, difficulty in falling asleep and poor digestion.

_____

_____

_____

_____

_____

_____

_____

_____

_____

_____

_____

48

Write about your feelings, emotions and thoughts

Do you have person that you can trust to talk with about your feelings, emotions and thoughts?

The other person may not need to say anything, but it is important that you talk about these things to get them out of your mind.

People need people. We are all social beings and we need each other to self-regulate, and to help us see ourselves from a different perspective.

Who are the people in your life that you can open up to about your feelings, emotions and thoughts?

_____

_____

_____

_____

_____

_____

_____

_____

_____

_____

_____

_____

_____

_____

Can you be totally open with those people or that person? If not, why not? Do you have a hard time trusting people?

_____

_____

_____

_____

_____

_____

_____

_____

_____

If you don't have anyone to share your thoughts and feelings with right now, describe the next steps you will take to find someone who can listen to you without judgment and with compassion.

_____

_____

_____

_____

_____

_____

_____

_____

_____

_____

_____

49

Go to a sanctuary

Are you a religious or spiritual person? When was the last time you went to a sanctuary to pray or meditate? Churches, temples, synagogues, mosques and even natural places of sanctuary can offer relief to someone in pain.

We often see that when people are faced with pain from a terminal disease such as cancer, they find meaning to deep questions in the spiritual realm. Pain is a common symptom of cancer, and there is scientific evidence that the sensations of pain get less intense if the person feels more supported and less threatened. If this experience helps people with cancer-related pain, it also helps people with other kinds of non-cancer pain.

You will only find out if you try it.

Write about your experiences in a place of sanctuary.

You may choose to go to a new place or to remember your experience the last time you went to a sanctuary.

Describe the thoughts that come to your mind, the sensations through your body, your sense of connection with a spiritual world.

50

Explore your fears and worries

"Fear is an instinctive reaction to a known threat. Worry is a recurring thought about the future with an attempt to avoid an even more uncomfortable feeling."
— Diane McIntosh and Jonathan Horowitz

All animals have a built-in fear system. It is important to fear danger, to protect ourselves from danger and predators. However, humans have another system that is not present in animals.

Animals don't worry about the future. They live in the present. Humans, however, have a sense of past, present and future, and therefore we have the capacity to worry about the future.

Most worries that we have will never materialize. So why do we worry so much?

Explore your fears and worries.

Make a list of your fears and another list of your worries.

_____

_____

_____

_____

_____

_____

_____

_____

Is there any correlation between your fears and worries and the intensity of your pain? Describe it.

_____

_____

_____

_____

_____

_____

_____

_____

_____

_____

_____

_____

_____

51

Walk in nature

Find a nature trail, a beach, a river or some other green space and go for a walk.

Notice what you see, hear and smell.

Also, notice if walking in nature has any influence on your mood, sense of calm or sleep.

Proven benefits of regular walking outdoors include lower mortality, lower risk of cancer, diabetes and depression. It improves sleep quality, sugar metabolism, blood circulation, lung function and muscle strength. It prevents dementia, obesity, arthritis, chronic pain, fibromyalgia and cardiovascular problems such as myocardial infarct or stroke. And, as a bonus, it boosts creativity and imagination.

Write about what you felt during and after your walk in nature and if there was any effect on your pain sensations.

52

What brings you a sense of achievement and pride?

Reflect on the things that you have achieved despite having pain. What are you most proud of?

The brain needs dopamine, which is a neurotransmitter released when we have a sense of pride and achievement. Dopamine is important in fighting the negative effects of chronic pain.

BE PROUD

I have seen many patients who, despite having chronic pain for many years, are able to achieve their goals and be proud of themselves.

On the other hand, I have seen people with chronic pain who are also achieving a lot in their lives, but they do not realize they have made a lot of progress, because their life is so clouded by pain.

It is important to acknowledge your achievements, even if they are something small, like being able to complete a task at home or crafting an art project.

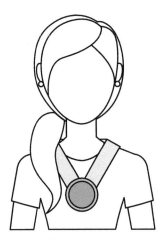

Chose one of your achievements and write about it.

53

List 10 things that calm you when you are agitated and stressed

If you are like me, when you are stressed, you forget all the strategies that bring you calm, and you end up doing things that stress you more.

I have created a list for myself of things to do in a stressful situation. For me, the 10 top things are:

1 Breathe.

2 Do not speak — keep my mouth shut until I can think with reason.

3 Offer a short prayer for wisdom in the moment.

4 Take some sips of water.

5 Get out of the environment for a few seconds.

6 Focus my attention on something else that is happening in parallel to the stressful situation.

7 Keep my eyes closed (if that is appropriate).

8 Remember that I am not responsible for what others say or do. I am only in control of what I say and do.

9 Put in my earbuds and listen to some calm music (if that is appropriate for the situation).

10 Go take a shower.

When I ask my patients what they can do to relieve stress, some of them will only think of the calming pills they have. This is not a good mechanism for coping with stress, as it creates a learned memory in the brain (synapse) that reinforces that pills are always a good solution to stress. Anti-anxiety pills are very quick to create physical tolerance (meaning higher doses are needed to cause the same effect) and dependence (which can result in withdrawal symptoms when you stop using the pills).

Write your own list of 10 strategies to cope with stress.

Do this exercise when you are calm and not stressed.

Keep your list close, so when a stressful situation arises, you can look at it and use some of these strategies to bring you calm.

_____

_____

_____

_____

_____

_____

_____

_____

_____

_____

_____

_____

_____

_____

_____

_____

_____

54

What kind of
physical activity relaxes you?

Many scientists have taken pictures of the brains of people in chronic pain. The images show that the most prominent areas of the brain that are activated are areas related to fear, sadness, memory, worry and emotions in general. It is also interesting that when they repeat these images in people with chronic pain who exercise regularly, these areas diminish and the person feels less pain.

We know that physical exercise is one of the best strategies to revert the changes that chronic pain causes in the pain system, not only in the brain, but also in the peripheral nerves, the spinal cord (where central sensitization starts), and even the immunological cells, hormones and microbiota in the guts.

Make a list of the top 10 physical activities that relax both your body and your mind.

55

What kind of music relaxes you?

> "Music hath charms to soothe a savage beast,
> to soften rocks, or bend a knotted oak."
> — William Congreve

Listening to, playing or creating music is a great exercise for the brain. A lot of scientific evidence shows that when we listen to music, our brain is active in many areas that counterbalance the sympathetic nerve system, the part of our autonomous system that responds to stress by releasing adrenaline and cortisol. By paying attention to music, the brain will activate the opposite system, the parasympathetic nervous system, which is the system that relaxes and promotes healing.

Also, listening to music has effects on the creativity, imagination and planning areas of the brain, which are areas that activate the top-down pain inhibitory pathways. The brain has an amazing capacity to create new synapses, and this is the main principle of neuroplasticity. Because the main mechanism of chronic pain is nociplastic pain (synapses that are constantly firing), we need to fight it with neuroplasticity. Therefore, listening and paying attention to music is a very effective way to revert neuroplastic changes in the brain.

Make a list of the top 10 music tracks (or music genres) that relax you.

Circle the one that you are going to listen to this week.

Make an effort to listen and pay attention to it. Try to memorize the lyrics or, if it doesn't have lyrics, try to identify the instruments and rhythm that is being played.

If you are able to play an instrument, practice more and try to compose a song.

56

What kind of setting relaxes you?

Finding a relaxing setting is very important for people who have chronic pain. This is a place of calm where they are able to activate their parasympathetic nervous system, which is important for healing. Because pain can be a strong stressor, the person with chronic pain constantly activates the opposite system, which is the sympathetic nervous system.

For this reason, it is important to identify a setting that relaxes you, so you can go there when you need it. This can be a place inside your home or outside. It can be driving through a mountain or sitting in a garden. It can be looking at a fireplace at home or touring an art gallery. It can be watching cat or baby videos on the internet, or going to the park and watching dogs playing.

Make a list of the top 10 settings that relax you.

Which one is your favorite, and why?

57

What kind of people calm you?

HOLDING HANDS EASES THE PAIN

In a very interesting laboratory experiment, scientists invited couples in a romantic relationship to test a hypothesis. They wanted to test the ability of the brain to reduce the interpretation of pain by being comforted by a partner. The study involved 22 couples who were exposed to various painful stimulations. Their brain waves were also monitored using an electroencephalograph.

At first, the participants were sitting together in the same room without holding their hands. Then they were holding hands. Finally, they were put in separate rooms. Both males and females were exposed to painful stimulus while the other person was not. What they found was that their brain waves related to focus and attention were in synchrony when they were together. And this synchrony became even stronger if they held hands.

What was most interesting was that during the phase when the couples were holding hands, the person reported that his/her pain was a lot less intense.

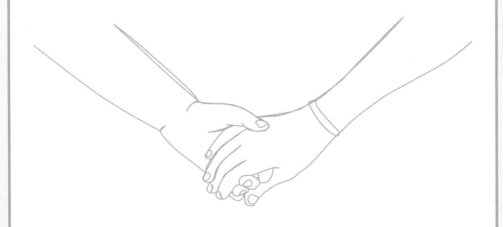

Make a list of the top three people who help you to relax and calm down.

_____

_____

_____

_____

_____

_____

What comforting words do they use when you are having a hard time?

_____

_____

_____

_____

_____

_____

What makes these people suitable to help you calm yourself?

_____

_____

_____

_____

_____

_____

_____

58

Are you a source of comfort to someone?

"Healing is the freedom to speak your mind."

— Carolyn Zepf

Can you remember the last time a friend called you because they needed a person to listen to and calm them?

Who was that person? What kind of problem did they bring to you? How did you react?

Reflect on the experience of being a source of comfort to someone.

What is the first thing you tell the other person when something bad happens to them?

_____

_____

_____

_____

_____

_____

What makes you a person that they can rely on?

_____

_____

_____

_____

_____

_____

How do you keep yourself under control when your friend is out of control?

_____

_____

_____

_____

_____

_____

_____

59

What are you grateful for?

The brain of a person living with chronic pain is in constant hypervigilance. It keeps scanning for threats and dangers, and trying to avoid situations that will aggravate the unpleasant feelings of pain. It is easy to forget or neglect important but less pressing aspects of life. And one that is commonly forgotten is the practice of being grateful.

Even in the presence of persistent pain, there are many other things that are happening around you for which you could be thankful. And practicing gratitude brings a sense of calm and peace.

What is gratitude to you? Can you define it?

How often are you grateful?

How do you express your gratitude?

What are you grateful for?

60

What physical exercises have you been able to do on a regular basis?

Exercise releases endorphins, the feel-good neurotransmitters, our endogenous opioids.

Try to achieve 150 minutes of exercise every week.

The benefits include improved mood, confidence, self-esteem, social interaction, building muscles and flexibility.

Make a list of the physical exercises you have been doing lately.

For each exercise, add a note about how you feel during and after the exercise routine.

TYPE OF EXERCISE	WHAT DOES IT DO FOR...			
	YOUR PAIN?	YOUR MOOD?	YOUR SLEEP?	YOUR OVERALL SENSE OF ACHIEVEMENT?

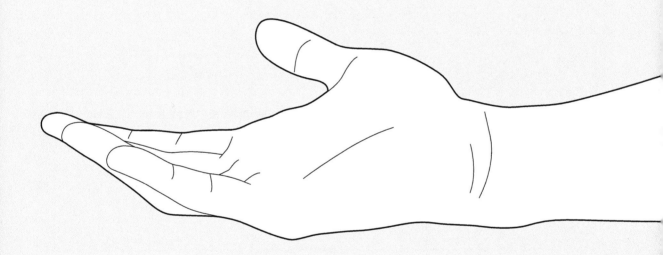

61

Self-care strategies

Take care of yourself. The things that you do to take care of your body and mind, whether big or small, are self-care. It is helpful to have self-care strategies you can turn to when pain is affecting your life.

Describe the top three self-care practices you do that help to alleviate your pain.

_____

_____

_____

_____

_____

_____

_____

_____

_____

_____

_____

_____

_____

_____

_____

_____

_____

_____

62

Positive experience

**"I am convinced that life is 10% what happens
to me and 96% how I react to it."**

— Scipio Africanus (236 to 183 BC)

Write about a positive situation that you have experienced in relation
to your pain.

_____

_____

_____

_____

_____

_____

_____

_____

_____

_____

_____

_____

_____

_____

_____

_____

_____

When was it?

_____

_____

_____

_____

What happened?

_____

_____

_____

_____

Who was involved?

_____

_____

_____

_____

Why was it a positive experience for you?

_____

_____

_____

_____

_____

63

Defeated by pain

**"Being defeated is often a temporary condition.
Giving up is what makes it permanent."**

—Marilyn vos Savant

Reflect about a time when you felt defeated by your pain.
What happened?

_____

_____

_____

_____

_____

_____

_____

_____

_____

_____

_____

_____

_____

_____

_____

_____

_____

_____

What was different about this time compared to other times?

_____

_____

_____

_____

_____

_____

_____

_____

_____

How did you bounce back?

_____

_____

_____

_____

_____

_____

_____

_____

_____

_____

_____

_____

64

A new treatment

Describe a new technique or treatment that you recently discovered that provided good pain relief. What was it?

Why did it help your pain?

_____

_____

_____

How did you first learn about this new treatment?

_____

_____

_____

How long did you feel the pain relief?

_____

_____

_____

Is this something you can do for yourself or do you need a clinician
to do it for you?

_____

_____

_____

What are your plans for continuing to use this treatment?

_____

_____

_____

_____

65

Positive affirmations

> **"I can be changed by what happens to me.**
> **But I refuse to be reduced by it."**
>
> — Maya Angelou

Do you believe in the power of positive affirmations? They do work!

Just as everyone's pain is different, what works for you as an affirmation may be different from what works for someone else. For example, some people with chronic pain need to be reminded that the pain they feel is real, but it is not a signal that something is broken or diseased.

Here are some examples of positive affirmations you can repeat to yourself when you are facing a difficult situation related to your pain, for example, during a pain flare-up.

- This will pass.

- I am strong.

- My body is not broken.

- I have the tools to conquer this pain.

- I always learn something useful with every new pain episode.

- The doctor is not concerned, so I should not be concerned either.

- I can move my body.

- Every injury heals.

- I refuse to be controlled by pain. I am in control.

- I am getting stronger, not weaker.

- I am unique and precious.

- I am learning how to retrain my pain pathways.

Write your own list of positive affirmations.

66

Your favorite distractions

Although sometimes it may be good to clear your mind of distractions (see Mind fasting, Day 45), purposeful distractions can be good for both acute and chronic pain.

Distraction doesn't mean neglecting necessary care; it doesn't mean distracting yourself instead of receiving treatment such as medication, injections or surgery. It is not supposed to be a replacement for therapy, but an addition or complementary treatment. People who use distraction techniques often find that as a result they need less medical treatment.

Many distraction techniques are free. Some can even be financially productive, like working, doing something for hire or producing something for sale.

Make a list of your favorite activities that distract you during a pain flare.

Relaxation or meditation

Pick your favorite relaxation or meditation technique. Describe it in detail, as if you were giving instructions to someone who has never practiced it before.

_____

_____

_____

_____

_____

_____

_____

_____

_____

_____

_____

_____

_____

_____

_____

_____

_____

_____

_____

_____

Self-love

What does self-love mean to you?

I certainly do not think it is spending lots of money on a spa, going on a shopping spree, staying at a luxurious hotel or eating in an expensive restaurant. These are examples of self-indulgence and may have serious financial consequences.

Self-love comprises strategies that you use to take care of yourself before you can take care of anyone else. If you have ever traveled by airplane, you will remember that they say to put the oxygen mask on yourself first, and then you can help those around you.

If you are running out of oxygen in your daily routine, how can you help others? You need to feed yourself with good nutrition and energy, especially if you have chronic pain.

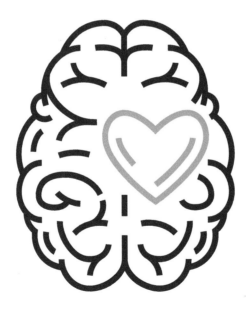

Make a list of your self-love strategies. Try to think of at least one strategy for each of these various areas of your life:

Nutrition

_____

_____

_____

Sleep

_____

_____

_____

Psychological

_____

_____

_____

Relationships

_____

_____

_____

Exercise

_____

_____

_____

_____

69

Advocate for yourself

Do you know how to advocate for yourself?

Reflect on how you advocate for yourself in the following situations:

- With a family member

- At work or at school

- At a medical appointment

Choose one situation in which you think you did well, when you were able to advocate for yourself and get tangible and meaningful results.

Write about one situation that went well.

_____

_____

_____

_____

_____

What did you do that worked well?

_____

_____

_____

_____

_____

_____

_____

Did you prepare before you met the person? How?

_____

_____

_____

_____

Did you take notes during the encounter?

_____

_____

_____

_____

_____

Did you ask questions?

_____

_____

_____

_____

_____

What would you do differently another time?

_____

_____

_____

_____

_____

70

One lifestyle change

If you have a healthy lifestyle, you are better equipped to manage your pain. Even small lifestyle modifications can have big results, both physically and mentally.

Areas where lifestyle changes can make a difference include:

- Exercise
- Sleep
- Stress management
- Smoking cessation
- Alcohol cessation
- Nutrition
- Mindfulness
- Socialization

Write about one lifestyle change that you have made to better manage your pain.

_____

_____

_____

_____

What was it?

_____

_____

_____

_____

_____

_____

How did it change your pain?

_____

_____

_____

_____

_____

_____

_____

71

Helpful online resources

The internet contains a lot of stuff, good and bad. Let's look for the good.

You can find various means of connecting with other people (individuals and groups), millions of educational websites, videos, books and blogs, all to help support you in your pain journey.

People don't need a personal computer any more, and many can access all the information using a smartphone. There are thousands of applications that can be downloaded and offer excellent resources at low cost or free of charge.

These can be applications on your smartphone, websites, blogs, groups, videos, audiobooks, e-books, portals and scientific papers. (I hope my YouTube channel will make your list!)

See https://www.youtube.com/@DrAndreaFurlan

Make a list of your top 10 online resources to manage your pain.

_____

_____

_____

_____

_____

_____

_____

_____

_____

_____

Pick one of these online resources and write about it in detail.

What do you like about it? How often to you access it? What does it do to your overall well-being?

_____

_____

_____

_____

_____

_____

_____

_____

_____

_____

_____

_____

72

Gratitude

No, you are not going to write a list of things that you are grateful for here. Instead, think about your favorite methods for practicing gratitude.

Reflect on a routine that you may have to express your gratitude. This might include prayers, a gratitude journal, a meeting with a friend or spouse to share what you are thankful for, an app, a meditation practice or something else.

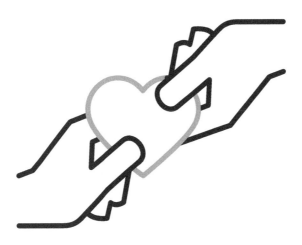

If you had to teach someone one method of expressing gratitude, what would it be? Describe your method.

What do you do?

How long does it take?

How often do you do this?

Why do you do it?

What does it do for you?

73

Lower your resting respiratory rate

We usually do not think about our breathing. But thinking about our breathing can be extremely helpful, especially when we are stressed, afraid and tense — all of which happens when we are faced with a pain flare.

Our lungs have an important function, to take in oxygen and to get rid of carbon dioxide. This exchange of gas happens at the alveoli.

The respiratory rate (RR), or breathing rate, is a measure of how much exchange we need to make. When we are moving our body, our muscles need more oxygen and will produce more carbon dioxide. The number of times in one minute that your chest or abdomen rises (the RR) will increase when we are moving. A resting respiratory rate should be around 12 to 20 breaths per minute.

When a person is calm and at rest, they should be able to lower the RR to 10 per minute, and in some occasions even lower, and still deliver enough oxygen to the whole body.

HOW TO MEASURE YOUR RESPIRATORY RATE

- Sit or lie down. Place one hand on the top of your chest or abdomen.

- Start a timer for 1 minute.

- Breathe normally.

- Count the number of times your chest or abdomen rises for the course of one minute.

- That number is your respiratory rate or RR. Write it down.

WHY REDUCE YOUR RR?

Being able to reduce your RR means that you are able to relax your body and mind. This will come in very handy when you face stressful situations, because the stress hormones make pain more intense and difficult to tolerate. The vagus nerve is a powerful nerve that controls many internal organs, including the lungs and respiration. When we intentionally control our breathing, we are activating the vagus nerve and the parasympathetic nervous system (the rest, digest and healing system).

Record your RR when you are calm and at rest. What is it?

Try to do a relaxation technique that involves calming your breath.

Are you able to lower your RR when you are calm?

How low can your RR go?

74

Silver lining

"Every cloud has a silver lining." — Proverb

A silver lining is a positive aspect of an otherwise negative situation. Nobody will say that having chronic pain is a good thing in itself. Pain is a sensation that is produced in the brain in response to danger, perceived or real. It is not normal to feel pleasure because you are suffering pain.

However, there are many people with chronic pain who have gained a better understanding of themselves, the meaning of their lives, their relationships, their goals or their spiritual connections because of their pain experience.

I once had a patient who had chronic pain for many years. She was married to a very powerful, dominant and wealthy husband. She had two adult children and had stopped her career when she got married to raise her family. She didn't have close friends or family around. She told us she was hiding her pain issues from her children so as not to bother them. She felt very lonely.

Her pain was mostly nociplastic, and our team helped her to overcome her frustrations and helplessness. When we discharged her from our clinic, her pain was almost completely gone. She said the best thing that happened to her was telling her daughter and son about her pain. The pain allowed her to reconnect with her children and she gained confidence and resilience.

Try to think of any positive perspective that you have gained from your pain journey. Describe at least one silver lining.

75

One goal that you have achieved

Sometimes you have to make a commitment to yourself and set goals for improvement or accomplishments. Setting goals, big or small, helps you to control your journey.

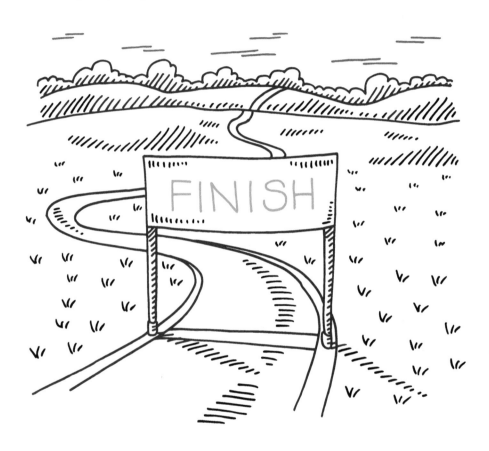

Describe a goal that you have achieved in your pain journey.

What was your goal?

Did you write it down?

Did you use the SMARTer technique to define your goal? (Specific, Measurable, Attainable, Time-bound, Evaluable, Revisable)

When did you achieve it?

Was it easier or harder than you expected?

How did you know when you achieved it?

How did you celebrate it?

76

Your small victories over pain

Many people have postponed things in their lives because they are waiting until the day when they will be pain free to do them. They don't realize that the pain might be persistent and stay for a long time in their lives. Before they realize it, they may have missed out on a lot of important aspects of life.

Being engaged with your life and what is important to you is part of the therapy for chronic pain. I often recommend Acceptance and Commitment Therapy (ACT) to my patients. It's a kind of psychological therapy that helps people to commit to what is important to them and to do it.

Let go of the rope!

Fighting the pain will only drain your energy.
Let it go and move toward what is important
and meaningful in your life.

Make a list of the small victories you have achieved despite living with chronic pain.

Write down your small victories — the things that are important to you, as a person, that you have done despite having chronic pain. This list might contain things that might sound tiny or small but, remember, you did them. What were they?

77

Overcoming fatigue

Fatigue is a very common symptom among people with chronic pain. Fatigue is different from being tired. Tiredness is improved with rest; fatigue is not. The person with fatigue usually feels very tired during the day and they can't sleep well. Because they have insomnia and sleep disturbances, it becomes a vicious cycle.

Fatigue is also a common side effect of many medications used to treat pain, including opioids, antidepressants, anticonvulsants, muscle relaxants and benzodiazepines.

What are your top 10 non-drug strategies that help you to overcome your fatigue? If you can't think of 10, you may want to do some research, attend webinars, read books and watch videos to learn them. The more techniques you have, the better, because they can be used in combination with each other to help you to overcome this symptom of fatigue.

Make a list of the top 10 strategies that help you overcome fatigue.

Recharging
our battery means
we have to stop,
rest and relax.

How do you recharge your battery?

Our brain needs time to process all the information that we absorb during the day. Our body needs time to rest and to heal from any injuries or damage and exposure to germs and diseases. That is why we sleep.

What is your favorite way to recharge?

What benefits does this recharging activity have on your mind?

How does it affect your muscles?

What benefits does it have on your overall quality of life?

Energy conservation

Energy conservation is about finding a balance between activity and rest.

All organs of our body consume energy to function. I mean "all organs," including the ones that you don't even think about, such as the skin, the guts and even the bones. People usually think their bones are inanimate, like rocks, but actually they are very alive, and bones also consume energy to repair themselves, to renew their cells and to reshape as we age.

So, how do you balance activity and rest? What is your favorite way?

Some examples are pacing yourself, planning ahead, making a to-do list, prioritizing your day, advocating for yourself, taking breaks at work.

What is your favorite way to conserve your energy? Describe it in detail.

80

Feeling guilty?

Reflect on any feelings of guilt you have that are associated with chronic pain.

Guilt is a natural emotion that happens to anyone, but those who have chronic pain may feel guilty because they can't participate in activities that they would do if they didn't have pain. They may feel that they are letting people down or think that they did something wrong that caused the pain.

Guilt is a complex emotion that is commonly associated with anxiety and depression. Depending on the impact of guilt in the person's life, they may need professional counseling to overcome and resolve their guilt.

The first step to overcome this emotion is to acknowledge its presence.

Write about your feelings of guilt.

_____

_____

_____

_____

_____

_____

_____

_____

_____

_____

_____

_____

_____

_____

_____

_____

_____

_____

_____

_____

_____

_____

_____

"Your journal is a place to channel rage on a page;
you can swear, win every argument, be messy
and incomprehensible." — Carolyn Zepf

81

Pleasure and joy

Finding pleasure and demonstrating joy does not mean that you are not in pain. Some people think that because a person is laughing and having a good time their pain is not real or they are faking their joy.

Yet the two can happen at the same time. There are small — and big — pleasures in life that bring you joy despite your chronic pain.

The fact that you are in pain does not mean you cannot feel pleasure, happiness and joy in your life.

Actually, while you respect and acknowledge the fact that you are in pain, you can and should pursue joyful moments.

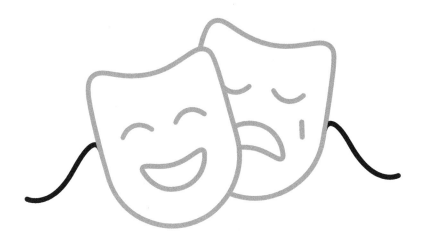

Write about the moments of pleasure that bring you joy.

What do they mean to you?

How do they help you to cope with your pain?

82

Your hobbies

A hobby is any activity that you do on a regular basis that is not for obligation or money. You do it just because you like it.

Make a list of hobbies or activities that you enjoy.

How do they help you cope with your pain?

_____

_____

_____

_____

_____

_____

_____

_____

If you don't have any hobbies, look at what your friends, family or
acquaintances are doing, or search the internet for inspiration. Then,
choose one hobby that you would like to develop and write about it.

_____

_____

_____

_____

_____

_____

_____

_____

_____

_____

_____

83

Uncertainties related to chronic pain

Everyone has thoughts of uncertainty related to their chronic pain. That uncertainty can cause fear.

The first step to lose the fear is to acknowledge its presence, then discuss it with someone who knows more in this area than you do.

Reflect on your uncertainties.

What don't you know about your pain?

_____

_____

_____

_____

_____

_____

_____

_____

_____

_____

_____

_____

_____

_____

_____

_____

Are your doctors uncertain about your pain treatments? How does that affect you?

_____

_____

_____

_____

_____

_____

_____

_____

_____

What fears do you have related to uncertainties in your future with chronic pain? Write a list, then review it and circle your three greatest fears.

_____

_____

_____

_____

_____

_____

_____

_____

_____

_____

_____

84

Feeling safe again

Think back to a time when you did not feel safe. It could be any period of your life, your childhood or young adult life, or your current situation.

WARNING

Write the first 10 words that come to mind when you think about not feeling safe.

Now reflect on how these emotions might be affecting your pain. Is there a connection between you not feeling safe and a flare of your chronic pain?

_____

_____

_____

_____

_____

_____

_____

_____

Think back to a time when you felt safe. Is there anything you can do or change to recall that feeling?

_____

_____

_____

_____

_____

_____

_____

_____

_____

_____

_____

_____

85

Tell your doctor

Some people are afraid of talking to their doctors or nurses about their pain. They think they will be judged, seen as a weak, drug-seeking, difficult patient, and that they will be labeled by the system.

Write a letter to your doctor. Tell him or her everything that you would like to tell them.

You don't need to show this letter to them. Nobody needs to read this letter. It is just an exercise for you to practice your conversation. Perhaps you can use some of this exercise in a future encounter with your doctor. Go prepared for the conversation. Ask relevant questions and explain your pain and quality of life to your doctor.

Dear Doctor,

86

Don't suffer because of lack of knowledge

How much do you know about your pain diagnosis? If you had to write an essay about your pain, what would you say?

Here is an opportunity to ask yourself how much you know. Try to answer the following questions about your pain diagnosis.

What kind of pain it is? Nociceptive, neuropathic, nociplastic or mixed?

_____

_____

_____

_____

_____

_____

_____

Who are the people most affected by this type of pain?

Females, males, people with obesity, people who use nicotine, alcohol or opioids? People with a previous history of childhood adversities?

_____

_____

_____

_____

_____

_____

_____

What are the symptoms associated with this pain?

Examples include numbness, muscle weakness, tremors, inflammation, sleep problem, depression, fatigue and poor concentration.

_____

_____

_____

_____

_____

How do doctors usually diagnose this type of pain?

_____

_____

_____

_____

_____

What are some evidence-based treatment strategies for this condition?

_____

_____

_____

_____

_____

What questions do you have for your doctor about your pain condition?

_____

_____

_____

_____

_____

_____

87

Lessons from a pain flare-up

Reflect on the last time you had a pain flare-up. Think of an episode
when your pain got worse for a period of time and went back to the
baseline again.

What were the triggers that contributed to this pain episode? Make a list.

What did you do during the pain flare?

What did you after the pain flare?

_____

_____

_____

_____

_____

Did you notice any stressor or behaviors that precipitated this pain flare?

_____

_____

_____

_____

_____

_____

_____

_____

_____

_____

_____

How much control did you have over this pain flare?

0   1   2   3   4   5   6   7   8   9   10

You may give a mark from 0 to 10, where 0 is feeling totally at the mercy of the pain and not able to do anything to lower its impact on your life, and 10 is feeling you were in control and had strategies to lower the impact of the pain in your life.

Dream catcher

In Native American tradition, a dream catcher is a handmade willow hoop with feathers and beads that protects a person from bad dreams.

Write about your dreams.

What do you often dream?

Which emotions do they stimulate?

What do you remember about your dreams?

Is there a recurrent theme to your dreams? A person? A place? A situation?

What you say matters

Reflect on the words that you often say about your life, about yourself, about the pain, about the doctors, about your family.

What we say can affect what we think, and how we and others see us. We cannot undo the words that we said. The word "unsay" doesn't exist.

Do you use curse language? If yes, why?

Do you use more negative or more positive sentences?

Do you often repeat a saying, a proverb, a sentence? What is it?

What message do you want to convey when you say what you say? That you are angry, frustrated, tired, unhappy, hopeless?

How do you think people around you feel when they hear you saying what you often say?

90

Meet yourself in the future

Imagine that you can travel through time and you have just landed 10 years in the future.

Write yourself a letter. What would you like to tell yourself in the future? What are the things that you have accomplished over the past 10 years?

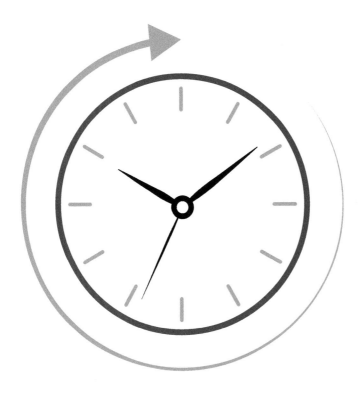

Dear future me,

Contact me on social media and tell me what you think of this journal.

 https://www.instagram.com/dr.andrea.furlan

 https://www.facebook.com/dr.andrea.furlan

 https://x.com/adfurlan

 https://www.youtube.com/@DrAndreaFurlan

OTHER BOOKS BY DR. ANDREA FURLAN

8 Steps to Conquer Chronic Pain:
A Doctor's Guide to Lifelong Relief

Library and Archives Canada Cataloguing in Publication
Title: You're unique & so is your pain : a daily reflections journal for lifelong well-being /
 Andrea Furlan, MD, PhD, PM&R.
Other titles: You are unique and so is your pain
Names: Furlan, Andrea (Andrea Dompieri), author.
Identifiers: Canadiana 20250112094 | ISBN 9780778807315 (softcover)
Subjects: LCSH: Chronic pain. | LCSH: Chronic pain—Treatment.
Classification: LCC RB127.5.C48 F87 2025 | DDC 616/.0472—dc23